HISTORICAL PERSPECTIVES
In Their Own Words

The Words of ANNE FRANK

Jagger Youssef

PowerKiDS press

Published in 2023 by The Rosen Publishing Group, Inc.
2544 Clinton Street, Buffalo, NY 14224

Portions of this work were originally authored by Caroline Kennon and published as *Anne Frank in Her Own Words.* All new material in this edition authored by Jagger Youssef.

Editor: Therese Shea
Book Design: Michael Flynn

Photo Credits: Cover https://commons.wikimedia.org/wiki/File:Anne_Frank_lacht_naar_de_schoolfotograaf.jpg; (series background) merrymuuu/Shutterstock.com; (fact box) Miloje/Shutterstock.com; p. 5 https://commons.wikimedia.org/wiki/File:Anne_Frank_passport_photo,_May_1942.jpg; p. 7 (Anne) https://commons.wikimedia.org/wiki/File:AnneFrank1940_crop.jpg; p. 7 (Otto) https://en.wikipedia.org/wiki/Otto_Frank#/media/File:Otto_Frank_(1961).jpg; p. 7 (Edith) https://en.wikipedia.org/wiki/Edith_Frank#/media/File:Edith_Frank_photo.jpg; p. 7 (Margot) https://commons.wikimedia.org/wiki/File:Margot_Frank_op_het_Joods_lyceum.jpg; p. 9 Kollawat Somsri/Shutterstock.com; p. 11 spatuletail/Shutterstock.com; p. 13 (house) Rob Atherton/Shutterstock.com; p.13 (bookcase) https://commons.wikimedia.org/wiki/File:AnneFrankHouse_Bookcase.jpg; p. 15 https://commons.wikimedia.org/wiki/File:Peter_van_Pels_2014-05-28_00-43.jpg; p. 16 https://en.wikipedia.org/wiki/File:Fritz_Pfeffer.jpg; p. 17 https://commons.wikimedia.org/wiki/File:Anne_Frank_House_Model.JPG; p. 19 Jerry Lampen/Reuters/Alamy; p. 21 https://commons.wikimedia.org/wiki/File:Presentatie_boek_Herinneringen_aan_Anne_Frank_van_Miep_Gies_in_het_Anne_Frankh,_Bestanddeelnr_933-9705.jpg; p. 22 Sergey Borzov/Shutterstock.com; p. 23 https://commons.wikimedia.org/wiki/File:Child_survivors_of_Auschwitz.jpeg; p. 25 Ronald Wilfred Jansen/Shutterstock.com; p. 27 https://commons.wikimedia.org/wiki/File:The_Liberation_of_Bergen-belsen_Concentration_Camp,_April_1945_BU4711_(cropped).jpg.

Library of Congress Cataloging-in-Publication Data

Names: Youssef, Jagger, author.
Title: The words of Anne Frank / Jagger Youssef.
Description: New York : PowerKids Press, [2023] | Series: Historical perspectives: in their own words | Includes index.
Identifiers: LCCN 2022025873 (print) | LCCN 2022025874 (ebook) | ISBN 9781642824544 (library binding) | ISBN 9781642824520 (paperback) | ISBN 9781642824551 (ebook)
Subjects: LCSH: Frank, Anne, 1929-1945--Juvenile literature. | Jews--Netherlands--Amsterdam--Biography--Juvenile literature. | Jewish children in the Holocaust--Netherlands--Amsterdam--Biography--Juvenile literature. | Amsterdam (Netherlands)--Biography--Juvenile literature.
Classification: LCC DS135.N6 F73967 2023 (print) | LCC DS135.N6 (ebook) | DDC 940.53/18092 [B]--dc23/eng/20220204
LC record available at https://lccn.loc.gov/2022025873
LC ebook record available at https://lccn.loc.gov/2022025874

Manufactured in the United States of America

CPSIA Compliance Information: Batch #CWPK23. For further information contact Rosen Publishing at 1-800-237-9932.

CONTENTS

EARLY LIFE

Annelies Marie Frank, known to the world as Anne Frank, was a young girl during World War II. However, she became one of the most powerful voices of the war, a conflict she didn't survive. Anne started a diary in 1942, when she was 13 years old. Through her honest and thoughtful words, people have come to understand what life was like for this Jewish teen during the **Holocaust**.

Anne and her family were German Jews. Anne was clearly aware of the hatred toward Jewish people at that time. The Franks' lives changed after Adolf Hitler, leader of the **Nazi** party, became German **chancellor** in 1933 and then president in 1934. Hitler and the Nazis wrongly blamed Jews for events such as World War I (1914–1918) as well as Germany's poor economy.

LOOKING BACK

Anne Frank was born in Frankfurt, Germany, on June 12, 1929. Her parents were Edith and Otto Frank. She had an older sister named Margot.

The Gift

On June 20, 1942, soon after receiving her diary, Anne wrote: "Writing in a diary is a really strange experience for someone like me. Not only because I've never written anything before, but also because it seems to me that later on neither I nor anyone else will be interested in the musings of a thirteen-year-old schoolgirl." She was wrong. Anne's writings later became world famous, read by millions of people.

This photograph of Anne was taken a month before her 13th birthday, when she received her diary.

Otto Frank recognized the dangers his family faced under Nazi control. In 1933, he moved from Germany to the city of Amsterdam in the Netherlands, where he set up a business. The rest of the Frank family soon followed. Anne later explained, "*Because we're Jewish, my father* ***immigrated*** *to Holland in 1933, where he became the managing director of the Dutch Opekta Company, which manufactures products used in making jam.*"

Amsterdam seemed welcoming. Anne began school and made friends of many religions and backgrounds. However, she wrote that many of their "*relatives in Germany were suffering under Hitler's anti-Jewish laws.*" In November 1938, the Nazis burned **synagogues** as well as Jewish homes and businesses in Germany. The event became known as Kristallnacht (Night of Broken Glass).

LOOKING BACK

Anne called the Netherlands "Holland." Many people still do, although Holland is a region of the Netherlands. Amsterdam is the capital city of the Netherlands.

Just a Kid

Like most young people, Anne had a lot of energy. She displayed a love for reading and writing in school. Her friend Hannah "Hanneli" Goslar said that Anne didn't like showing other people what she wrote. Anne was also always ready to have fun. She played hopscotch, tag, and Ping-Pong. One of her favorite pranks was to throw water from her apartment building window onto people on the street below.

These photos show Anne, her parents, and her sister Margot. The Franks were among 300,000 Jewish people who left Germany between 1933 and 1939.

THE WAR BEGINS

On September 1, 1939, Germany invaded Poland, beginning World War II. Germany then invaded Norway, Denmark, and the Netherlands. After five days of fighting in May 1940, the Netherlands surrendered. Anne was 10 years old.

Anne later wrote in her diary: "After May 1940 the good times were few and far between. . . . Our freedom was severely restricted by a series of anti-Jewish decrees . . . . You couldn't do this and you couldn't do that, but life went on."

The Nazis destroyed property and put up signs on businesses that said: "No Jews Allowed." Jewish children had to go to Jewish schools. Anne made friends at her new school, though. She played the game Monopoly, read books, and visited the Jewish ice-cream shop.

LOOKING BACK

Jews weren't the only targets of Nazi violence. Other groups that were singled out were the **Romany**, **Slavs**, and people with mental and physical differences.

Discriminating Decrees

As in other Nazi-controlled territories, Jews in Amsterdam were required to follow certain decrees, or orders. Anne recorded some of the decrees: They had to wear a yellow star. They couldn't use streetcars. They could only shop between the hours of 3 p.m. and 5 p.m. They weren't allowed to walk in parks, use public swimming pools, or go to movies or plays. They had to turn in their bicycles too.

Jewish people in the Netherlands had to sew badges like this on their clothing during World War II. Jood is Dutch for "Jew."

ANNE'S GIFT

June 12, 1942, was Anne's 13th birthday. Her parents gave her a small notebook with a red-and-white plaid cover. Anne had seen it in a store and admired it. She used it as a diary, calling it "Kitty" and pretending it was a friend. She wrote: *"I'll begin from the moment I got you, the moment I saw you lying on the table among my other birthday presents."*

As the pressures of the war grew and the difficulties for Jewish people worsened, Anne's diary became even more important to her. Their home in Amsterdam became less safe every day. As Anne wrote to Kitty in her diary about their troubles, her father worried about how to help their family, once again in danger.

LOOKING BACK

Besides her diary writings, Anne Frank collected quotes from her favorite books and wrote her own short stories.

An Important Birthday

Otto and Edith Frank tried to make Anne's 13th birthday special to make up for the scary world their daughter was living in. They threw a party for her and her friends. Since Jews couldn't go to the movie theater, they invited Anne's friends over to watch a movie. They wanted to make sure that Anne and Margot lead as normal of a life as possible during the war.

This stamp shows Anne's diary as well as what her handwriting looked like.

THE SECRET PLAN

In the summer of 1942, Jewish people in Germany-controlled Netherlands began to be deported, or forced out of the country. Margot was ordered to a work camp. Otto and Edith acted quickly to save their family.

Anne wrote on July 5, 1942: "A few days ago, as we were taking a stroll around our neighborhood square, Father began to talk about going into hiding. He said it would be very hard for us to live cut off from the rest of the world."

Anne had questions: "When, where, how . . .? These were questions I wasn't allowed to ask, but they still kept running through my mind."

On July 6, 1942, the Franks moved into a hidden apartment Anne called the "secret **annex**." Anne and her family spent the next two years there.

LOOKING BACK

It's believed about 28,000 Jews hid in the Netherlands, as the Franks did.

Into the Annex

The Frank family left home early in the morning wearing many layers of clothes. Anne said it "looked as if we were going off to spend the night in a refrigerator." She explained that this was a clever way of taking as many clothes to the annex as they could: "No Jew in our situation would dare leave the house with a suitcase full of clothes." The authorities would know immediately that they were trying to escape.

This is the house that held the Franks' secret annex. A bookcase was built to hide the entrance.

SHARING SPACE

Another family, the Van Pels, moved into the annex a week later. Hermann van Pels was Otto Frank's business partner. He brought his wife, Auguste, and their son, Peter. Anne used pseudonyms, or fake names, in her writing in case she published her diary someday. She called this family the Van Daans.

Life in the annex wasn't easy. There was limited hot water, and they had to be very quiet. Anne remained cheerful: "I don't think I'll ever feel at home in this house, but that doesn't mean I hate it. It's more like being on vacation. . . . The Annex is an ideal place to hide in. It may be damp and lopsided, but there's probably not a more comfortable hiding place in all of Amsterdam. No, in all of Holland."

LOOKING BACK

The building with the secret annex was located on a canal in Amsterdam called the Prinsengracht.

Families Torn Apart

Some Jewish parents thought their children would have a better chance of survival if they were sent to live with Christian families, in convents, or to orphanages. Some children had their hair dyed in an attempt to make them look less Jewish. Many were given new names as well. Many of these children survived the war, but never found their parents or families again.

Peter van Pels was 16 years old when he and his parents entered the secret annex.

In November 1942, another person joined the Franks. Fritz Pfeffer was a dentist and friend of the family. Anne gave him the pseudonym Albert Dussel. He shared a room with Anne. She wrote, "I'm not exactly delighted at having a stranger use my things, but you have to make sacrifices for a good cause."

Anne began to notice that Pfeffer kept a lot of food to himself, storing bread, cheese, and other foods away from the rest of the group. She grew angry with him: "It's absolutely disgraceful that Dussel, whom we've treated with such kindness and whom we took in to save from destruction, should stuff himself behind our backs and not give us anything. After all, we've shared all we had with him!"

Fritz Pfeffer

LOOKING BACK

It's believed that Anne took the name she wrote to in her diary, Kitty, from a character in books she loved, the Joop ter Heul book series.

Thoughts of Others

Anne feared for friends who didn't have a secret annex: "We're so fortunate here, away from the turmoil. We wouldn't have to give a moment's thought to all this suffering if it weren't for the fact that we're so worried about those we hold dear, whom we can no longer help. . . . I get frightened myself when I think of close friends who are now at the mercy of the cruelest monsters ever to stalk the earth. And all because they're Jews."

This model shows the setup of the secret annex, which was connected to Otto Frank's business.

ON EDGE

Like any young person, Anne had her struggles, but she had them while in hiding and in the middle of a war. She turned to her diary: "It's not easy trying to behave like a model child with people you can't stand, especially when you don't mean a word of it."

Anne wasn't the only one who felt restless: "Relationships here in the Annex are getting worse all the time. We don't dare open our mouths at mealtime (except to slip in a bite of food), because no matter what we say, someone is bound to resent it or take it the wrong way . . . Sometimes I'm afraid my face is going to sag with all this sorrow and that my mouth is going to permanently droop at the corners. The others aren't doing any better."

LOOKING BACK

Anne made up pseudonyms for her family too. Margot was Betty Robin; Otto was Frederik Robin; Edith was Nora Robin; and she was Anne Robin.

Approaching Menace

Anne wrote about the danger she felt: "I see the eight of us in the Annex as if we were a patch of blue sky surrounded by menacing black clouds. The perfectly round spot on which we're standing is still safe, but the clouds are moving in on us, and the ring between us and the approaching danger is being pulled tighter and tighter. We're surrounded by darkness and danger."

Anne described going up to the attic of the annex to breathe fresh air each morning. She'd look out at this chestnut tree, which lived until 2010 when it blew over.

ARRESTED

In July 1944, Anne felt encouraged by news: *"Now I'm getting really hopeful, now things are going well at last. . . . An attempt has been made on Hitler's life."* However, on August 4, 1944, Nazi officers forced their way into the secret annex and arrested the Franks and the others.

The Franks were questioned, jailed, and sent to the Westerbork camp in northeastern Netherlands. They were placed in the punishment **barracks** for Jews who had gone into hiding. Anne, her sister, and her mother were put to work. Anne once again saw the positive side—she could spend time outside. But in September 1944, the eight people from the secret annex were sent by train to Auschwitz, a **concentration camp** in Poland.

LOOKING BACK

Miep Gies and Bep Voskuijl found Anne's diary among the belongings left behind. The last entry was August 1, 1944.

More Trouble

The people hiding in the secret annex had needed food and other supplies. Trusted friends had helped them. After the discovery of the annex, these people faced trouble as well. Johannes Kleiman and Victor Kugler were arrested and jailed. Jan and Miep Gies and Bep Voskuijl were questioned, but let go. It's believed that someone told the German secret police, called the Gestapo, about the secret annex, but no one knows who.

Jan and Miep Gies in 1987

Miep Gies and Bep Voskuijl were employees of Otto Frank's company. Anne was especially close with Bep. They'd often whisper to each other.

AUSCHWITZ

Prisoners were packed into trains to Auschwitz. More than 1,000 prisoners were on the train that carried the Franks for three days. Crowded conditions left no room to lie down. Those who were sick went directly to gas chambers to be killed. The others had their heads shaved, and numbers were **tattooed** on their arms. There was little to eat and only dirty water to drink. Anne was in charge of giving out bread in her barracks.

LOOKING BACK

Another woman who was at Auschwitz with Anne remembered her resourcefulness and charm. Anne was a leader and shared what she could spare.

Tragic Numbers

Between 1940 and 1945, around 1 million Jewish people were killed in Auschwitz. The largest gas chamber could hold 2,000 people at one time. Prisoners were locked in this room and poisoned with deadly gas. Some prisoners were used in medical experiments. Others killed themselves by touching the electric fence that surrounded the camp. On January 27, 1945, the Soviet army entered Auschwitz and freed the remaining prisoners, most of whom were ill and dying.

In the annex, Anne had written: "I am young and strong and am living a great adventure; I am still in the midst of it and can't grumble the whole day long. I have been given a lot, a happy nature, a great deal of cheerfulness and strength." She needed this strength in Auschwitz.

This photo shows children at Auschwitz who survived the camp's terrible conditions.

BERGEN-BELSEN

On November 1, 1944, Anne and Margot were taken to a camp in Germany, Bergen-Belsen. There they slept in crowded tents at first. Their tent collapsed in a thunderstorm. Though they later moved into barracks, less and less food was given out as time went on.

Anne and Margot met people they had known from other camps and schoolmates from their life in Amsterdam, which now seemed so far away. Talking with them was their only comfort. They worried about their parents.

Edith Frank died from starvation at Auschwitz on January 6, 1945. She was found with bread that she was saving for the rest of her family. Both Frank sisters grew weak by early 1945 and became sick with **typhus**.

LOOKING BACK

More than 50,000 people died in Bergen-Belsen, tens of thousands in the first months of 1945. One survivor called it "hell on Earth."

Horrific History

The Bergen-Belsen camp was a prisoner-of-war (POW) camp at first. As **Allied** forces marched into Germany in late 1944 and early 1945, Bergen-Belsen was used as a camp for thousands of Jewish prisoners moved from other sites. In July 1944, there were around 7,300 prisoners at Bergen-Belsen. The camp population rose to over 60,000 by April 1945. The crowded conditions meant days without food and quickly spreading diseases.

This is a view of the Bergen-Belsen concentration camp after it was liberated in 1945.

ANNE'S DEATH

In February 1945, Hanneli Goslar, a friend from Amsterdam, learned Anne was in a nearby section of Bergen-Belsen, on the other side of a fence. The Goslar family was going to be exchanged for German prisoners of war. Hanneli later remembered, "A German was in a watchtower at the top of the fence. He wouldn't have asked a lot. He just would have shot me. I wasn't allowed to come near the fence. Not only me, but Anna [Anne] too." The girls risked their lives to speak, whispering through the fence.

Anne and Margot grew weaker from their sickness and the terrible conditions. They died in February 1945 and were buried in an unknown grave with many others. Allied forces freed surviving prisoners at Bergen-Belsen two months later, in April 1945.

LOOKING BACK

Hanneli threw food to Anne over the fence, but another prisoner took it. She returned with more food. This time, Anne caught it. That was the last time the two saw each other.

Guilty

The Nazis were responsible for killing about 6 million Jews. In her diary, Anne said she didn't think the war was only Hitler's fault: "I don't believe that the big men . . . alone are guilty of the war. Oh no, the little man is just as guilty, otherwise the peoples of the world would have risen in revolt long ago! There's in people simply an urge to destroy." She believed everyone has a responsibility to stand up to evil.

A gravestone is placed in Bergen-Belsen to honor the Frank sisters. But it doesn't mark the exact location of their grave.

HER MEMORY LIVES ON

Of the eight people in the secret annex, Otto Frank was the only one to survive. He knew that Edith had died. Back in Amsterdam, he met two sisters who had been at Bergen-Belsen. They told him about Anne and Margot's deaths.

Miep Gies gave Anne's diary to Otto. He said, "I had no idea of the depths of her thoughts and feelings." He later published it. Since then, the book, in English called *The Diary of a Young Girl*, has sold more than 30 million copies and has been translated into more than 70 languages. Anne's ideas and experiences have moved countless people and inspired them to stand against hatred. Anne wrote, "I want to go on living, even after my death!" Her diary made this desire a reality.

LOOKING BACK

On May 7, 1945, Germany officially surrendered to Allied forces, and Japan surrendered on September 2, ending World War II.

Visiting the Secret Annex

In the mid-1950s, the secret annex—and the building it was in—was in danger of being torn down. Many had read Anne's diary by this time. People raised money to save the place where she and her family had hid. It became the Anne Frank House, a museum where visitors can see where Anne lived and wrote. Otto also started the International Youth Centre to teach young people about the dangers of **discrimination** and hate.

Timeline of Anne Frank's Life

1929 Anne Frank is born in Germany.

1933 Hitler rises to power in Germany.
Otto Frank moves to Amsterdam.

1934 Anne and the rest of her family move to Amsterdam.

1939 World War II begins.

1942 Anne receives a diary for her birthday in June.
The family goes into hiding, along with the Van Pels family, in July.
Fritz Pfeffer joins them in November.

1944 The secret annex is discovered in August.
Anne and the rest of her family are taken to Westerbork.
All are taken to Auschwitz in September.
Anne and Margot are taken to Bergen-Belsen in November.

1945 In January, Edith Frank dies. Auschwitz is liberated. Otto Frank is freed.
Anne and Margot die of typhus in February.
Bergen-Belsen is liberated in April.
Germany surrenders to the Allies in May.

1947 Anne's diary is published.

1960 The Anne Frank House opens to visitors.

GLOSSARY

Allied: Having to do with the Allies, a group of nations in World War II (including England and the United States) that opposed the Axis nations (including Germany and Japan).

annex: A building that has been added on to another building.

barracks: A temporary housing situation.

chancellor: The chief minister of government in some kinds of democracies.

concentration camp: One of the prison camps used for holding and killing prisoners in Nazi Germany.

discrimination: Unfairly treating people unequally because of their race or beliefs.

Holocaust: The mass murder of the Jews by the Nazis and their supporters during World War II.

immigrate: To come to a country to live there.

Nazi: Having to do with the German political party led by Hitler during World War II. Also, a member of the German army under the leadership of Adolf Hitler.

Romany: A traveling people who originated in northern India and now live mostly in south and southwest Asia, Europe, and North America.

Slav: Someone from eastern Europe or northwestern Asia who speaks one of the Slavic languages.

synagogue: A temple or a house of prayer for Jewish people.

tattoo: To mark the skin with a permanent design.

typhus: A disease that causes fever, headaches, rashes, and more and is spread by ticks and fleas carried by rodents.

FOR MORE INFORMATION

Books

Croy, Anita. *Anne Frank*. New York, NY: Lucent Press, 2020.

Krensky, Stephen. *Anne Frank*. New York, NY: DK Publishing, 2019.

Woodward, Kay. *The Life of Anne Frank*. Buffalo, NY: Firefly Books, 2020.

Websites

Anne Frank
www.annefrank.org/en/anne-frank/
Visit this website connected to the Anne Frank House museum to learn about her and the secret annex.

Anne Frank
www.jewishvirtuallibrary.org/jsource/biography/frank.html
See Anne Frank in the only existing film footage of her.

Anne Frank Biography
encyclopedia.ushmm.org/content/en/article/anne-frank-biography
The U.S. Holocaust Memorial Museum has information about Anne and other children who suffered during the Holocaust.

INDEX